First World War
and Army of Occupation
War Diary
France, Belgium and Germany

34 DIVISION
Divisional Troops
Divisional Cyclist Company
10 January 1916 - 31 May 1916

WO95/2445/2

The Naval & Military Press Ltd
www.nmarchive.com
Published in association with The National Archives

Published by

The Naval & Military Press Ltd

Unit 10 Ridgewood Industrial Park,

Uckfield, East Sussex,

TN22 5QE England

Tel: +44 (0) 1825 749494

www.naval-military-press.com

www.nmarchive.com

This diary has been reprinted in facsimile from the original. Any imperfections are inevitably reproduced and the quality may fall short of modern type and cartographic standards.

© Crown Copyright
Images reproduced by permission of The National Archives, London, England, 2015.

Contents

Document type	Place/Title	Date From	Date To
Miscellaneous	WO95/2445/2		
Miscellaneous	34 Div Cyclists		
Heading	34th Division Divl Troops 34th Divl Cyclists Jan-May 1916		
Miscellaneous	34th Divl. Cyclists Vol I Jan 16 May 16		
War Diary	Sutton Veny	10/01/1916	10/01/1916
War Diary	Southampton	10/01/1916	10/01/1916
War Diary	Le Havre	11/01/1916	11/01/1916
War Diary	St Omer	12/01/1916	12/01/1916
War Diary	Arques	20/01/1916	20/01/1916
War Diary	Estaires	23/01/1916	23/01/1916
Miscellaneous	34th Div Cyclists Vol 3		
War Diary	Bois Grenier	11/03/1916	11/03/1916
War Diary	Croix Du Bac	14/03/1916	14/03/1916
War Diary	Armentieres	15/03/1916	15/03/1916
War Diary	La Boudrelle	01/03/1916	14/03/1916
War Diary	Croix Du Bac	14/03/1916	11/04/1916
War Diary	Sec. Bois	12/04/1916	12/04/1916
War Diary	Saint Martin	13/04/1916	18/04/1916
War Diary	Rebergues	19/04/1916	01/05/1916
War Diary	St. Martin Au Laert	02/05/1916	05/05/1916
War Diary	Bresle	06/05/1916	08/05/1916
War Diary	Bresle And Behencourt	09/05/1916	09/05/1916
War Diary	Behencourt	10/05/1916	11/05/1916
War Diary	Behencourt And Beaucourt	12/05/1916	12/05/1916
War Diary	Beaucourt	13/05/1916	31/05/1916

WO95/2445/2

34 Div Cyclists

3TH DIVISION
DIVL TROOPS

34TH DIVL CYCLISTS
JAN - MAY 1916

34th Brit: Gelatin
vol I

JAN.

Jan -16
May -16

Army Form C. 2118.

WAR DIARY
INTELLIGENCE SUMMARY.
(Erase heading not required.)

34TH DIVISIONAL COMPANY, ARMY CYCLIST CORPS.

Instructions regarding War Diaries and Intelligence Summaries are contained in F. S. Regs., Part II. and the Staff Manual respectively. Title pages will be prepared in manuscript.

Place	Date	Hour	Summary of Events and Information	Remarks and references to Appendices
Sutton Veny	10/1/16	3 pm	Entrained for active service	
Southampton	10/1/16	7 pm	Embarked	
Le Havre	11/1/16	2 pm	Landed & entrained at midnight for St. Omer.	
St Omer	12/1/16	6 pm	Company went into billets in farm houses round Le Nieppe	
Arques	20/1/16	1 pm	Inspection by General Joffre	
Estaires	23/1/16	2 pm	Company went into billets in farm houses 300 yards N.E of Estaires town.	

W.E. Topp Capt
Comdg. 34th D.C.C.

34 DW
Eyebolts
Vol 3

WAR DIARY
or
INTELLIGENCE SUMMARY.

(Erase heading not required.)

34TH. DIVISIONAL COMPANY, ARMY CYCLIST CORPS.

Army Form C. 2118.

Place	Date	Hour	Summary of Events and Information	Remarks and references to Appendices
Bois Grenier	11/3/16		Commenced work putting up barbed wire entanglements, triangular shape, near Tramway Farm in front of 2nd line defences. The work was carried out at various times during the month. On the 16th inst, one man was killed whilst working.	
Croix Du Bac	14/3/16	3p	Company moved into billets in farm houses on the Croix Du Bac – Estaires road quite close to Croix Du Bac.	
Armentières	15/3/16		Company was employed digging trenches at Rue Allee at various times during the month. This work was commenced on the 15/3/16.	

Signed,
CAPTAIN.
Commdg. 34th. Div. Cyclists.

Sheet 1. Volume 3.

Army Form C. 2118.

Instructions regarding War Diaries and Intelligence Summaries are contained in F. S. Regs., Part II. and the Staff Manual respectively. Title pages will be prepared in manuscript.

WAR DIARY
or
INTELLIGENCE SUMMARY.
(Erase heading not required.)

**34TH. DIVISIONAL COMPANY,
ARMY CYCLIST CORPS.**

Place	Date	Hour	Summary of Events and Information	Remarks and references to Appendices
LA BOUDRELLE	1/3/16	9am	Weather:- Dull. Company employed building Rifle Butt for Snipers range at DIVISIONAL INSTRUCTION SCHOOL. Worked in two reliefs, each relief consisting of 45 N.C.Os & men. Party of 2 N.C.Os & 15 men employed in draining Cyclists Camp.	
"		11am & 2pm	Officers attended demonstrations by MAJOR DODSON at the DIVISIONAL INSTRUCTION School in the use of Smoke bombs	
			Admissions to Hospital NIL Discharges from Hospital NIL Evacuations NIL.	
"	2/3/16		Weather:- Fine	
		9am	Work on Rifle Butt continued by same reliefs. 1 Officer & Company SNIPERS went up to the TRENCHES to-day for instruction.	
			Admissions to Hospital 2 men Discharges from hospital NIL Evacuations NIL	
"	3/3/16		Weather:- Rain.	
		9am	Work on Rifle Butt continued by same reliefs. Officers attended a lecture by MAJOR DODSON in the Mess on Smoke bombs.	
		2pm		
		6pm	SNIPERS returned to Company for duty	
			Admissions to Hospital NIL Discharges from hospital NIL Evacuations NIL	

Sheet No. 2   Volume 3.

Army Form C. 2118.

WAR DIARY
or
INTELLIGENCE SUMMARY.
(Erase heading not required.)

34TH DIVISIONAL COMPANY,
ARMY CYCLIST CORPS.

Place	Date	Hour	Summary of Events and Information	Remarks and references to Appendices
LA BOUDRELLE	4/3/16	9 a.m.	Weather:- Rain & sleet. Company furnished the following fatigue parties:- 2 Officers and 50 N.C.Os & men at III Corps Coal Dump, BAC. ST. MAUR. 1 Officer and 30 men at R.E yard ARMENTIERES. 1 N.C.O and 10 men at SAILLY BRICK FIELDS. 6 men working under C.R.E. These parties worked until 4 p.m. Haversack rations were taken. Admissions to Hospital 1 N.C.O & 2 men. Discharges from hospital NIL. Evacuations NIL.	
-"-	5/3/16	9 a.m.	Weather:- Rain & Snow. Owing to bad weather work on RIFLE BUTT was postponed for the day. Admissions to Hospital 1 man. Discharges from Hospital 2 men. Evacuations NIL.	
-"-	6/3/16	9 a.m.	Weather:- Fair. Work continued on Rifle Butt by relief, all day.	
		9 a.m. to 5 p.m.	Party of 20 N.C.Os were employed preparing Trenches &c at the Divisional Instruction School for Trench Mortar Demonstration. 3rd issue of ANTI-GAS HELMETS today. 1st issue returned to store. Admissions to Hospital 1 Officer. Discharges from Hospital NIL. Evacuated 1 man.	

(LIEUT. J. WYNNE-HARLEY)

Sheet 3 Volume 3

Army Form C. 2118.

WAR DIARY
or
INTELLIGENCE SUMMARY.
(Erase heading not required.)

**34TH DIVISIONAL COMPANY,
ARMY CYCLIST CORPS.**

Instructions regarding War Diaries and Intelligence Summaries are contained in F. S. Regs., Part II. and the Staff Manual respectively. Title pages will be prepared in manuscript.

Place	Date	Hour	Summary of Events and Information	Remarks and references to Appendices
LA BOUDRELLE	7/3/16	9 a.m. to 5 p.m.	Weather:- Stormy. Work on Rifle Butt continued, by reliefs, all day. Party of 1 N.C.O & 20 men employed draining Camp. Admissions to Hospital 2 men Discharges from Hospital 1 man Evacuations NIL	
" "	8/3/16	9 a.m.	Weather:- Snow & Sleet. Work on Rifle Butt continued and finished at 6 p.m. 4 N.C.Os attached to 18th Pioneer Bn. N.F. for instruction in wiring. Admissions to Hospital NIL Discharges from Hospital NIL Evacuations 1 man	
" "	9/3/16	9 a.m. to 5 p.m.	The 4 N.C.Os attached to 18th N.F. gave demonstrations in Camp to the Company on the erection of barbed wire entanglements. Weather to-day:- Frost followed by steady thaw. Admissions to Hospital 1 man Discharges from Hospital NIL Evacuations NIL	
" "	10/3/16	9 a.m. to 5 p.m.	Company employed putting up BARBED WIRE ENTANGLEMENTS in Camp for practical purposes. Weather to-day:- Fair. Admissions to Hospital NIL Discharges from Hospital 1 N.C.O & 1 man Evacuations NIL	

Sheet No. 4 Volume 3.

Army Form C. 2118.

Instructions regarding War Diaries and Intelligence Summaries are contained in F.S. Regs., Part II. and the Staff Manual respectively. Title pages will be prepared in manuscript.

WAR DIARY
or
INTELLIGENCE SUMMARY.
(Erase heading not required.)

34TH. DIVISIONAL COMPANY,
ARMY CYCLIST CORPS.

Place	Date	Hour	Summary of Events and Information	Remarks and references to Appendices
LA BOUDRELLE	11/3/16	9 a.m. to 1 p.m.	PLATOONS paraded under Platoon Commanders for the following inspections:— BICYCLES, RIFLES, CLOTHING and EQUIPMENT.	
		2-30 p.m. to 5 p.m.	MUSKETRY and BAYONET FIGHTING.	
		7-30 p.m.	A party of 1 Officer, 2 N.C.Os & 16 men proceeded to TRAMWAY FARM near BOIS GRENIER to commence work of erecting a barbed wire entanglement, triangular shape, in front of BOIS GRENIER LINE TRENCH. Started work on triangle at 10-30 p.m. and continued until 2-30 A.M. 12/3/16. Party returned to billets 3-30 A.M. 12/3/16. Parties belonging to 18th PIONEER Bn. N.F. were engaged on similar work on our left. Weather to-day:— FINE Admissions to Hospital:— NIL Discharges from Hospital NIL Evacuations NIL	
	12/3/16	9 a.m. to 4-30 p.m.	Platoons paraded under Platoon Commanders for drill from 9 a.m. till 1 p.m. Lectures were given on MAP reading and the Compass from 2-30 p.m. till 4-30 p.m.	
		7-30 p.m.	1 Officer, 2 N.C.Os and 27 men proceeded to TRAMWAY FARM to continue with work on TRIANGLE. Commenced work 10-30 p.m. finished work 2-30 A.M. 13/3/16. Party returned to billets 3-30 A.M. 13/3/16. Admissions to Hospital 1 man Discharges from Hospital NIL Evacuations NIL. Weather to-day:— Very Fine	

Sheet No. 5 Volume 3.

Army Form C. 2118.

WAR DIARY
or
INTELLIGENCE SUMMARY.

34th. DIVISIONAL COMPANY,
ARMY CYCLIST CORPS.

(Erase heading not required.)

Place	Date	Hour	Summary of Events and Information	Remarks and references to Appendices
LA BOUDRELLE	13/3/16	9 a.m.	Company employed preparing for move to new billets	
		2 p.m.	— " — " — " — " — " — " —	
		7-30 p.m.	A party of 1 N.C.O & 10 men were employed all day at new billets erecting Cook house Latrines, & Incinerators.	
			1 Officer 2 N.C.Os & 20 men proceeded to TRAMWAY FARM to continue work on triangle Commenced work 10 p.m. finished work 2-30 A.M. 13/3/16. Party returned to billets	
		3-30 A.M.	Weather :- FINE	
			Admissions to Hospital Nil. Discharges from Hospital Nil. Evacuations 1 man.	
— " —	14/3/16	8 A.M.	A working party of 1 Officer, 5 N.C.Os & 45 men proceeded to ERQUINGHEM for work under R.E. III Corps. TRENCHING. Party returned to new billets at 3 p.m.	
CROIX DU BAC	14/3/16	3 p.m.	Company moved into billets in farm houses on the CROIX DU BAC — ESTAIRES road quite close to CROIX DU BAC	
			Weather :- FINE	
			Admissions to Hospital :- NIL Discharges from hospital NIL Evacuations NIL	

Sheet No. 6 VOLUME 3

Army Form C. 2118.

WAR DIARY
or
INTELLIGENCE SUMMARY.

34TH DIVISIONAL COMPANY,
ARMY CYCLIST CORPS.

(Erase heading not required.)

Instructions regarding War Diaries and Intelligence Summaries are contained in F. S. Regs., Part II. and the Staff Manual respectively. Title pages will be prepared in manuscript.

Place	Date	Hour	Summary of Events and Information	Remarks and references to Appendices
Croix-Du-Bac	15/3/16	3 a.m.	Party of 2 Officers 7 N.C.Os and 43 men proceeded to RUE ALLEE for TRENCHING work	
		6 p.m. to 7.45 p.m.	113 yards of trench dug 2½ ft wide x 2 feet deep.	
		9.30 a.m.	Party returned to billets.	
		7.30 p.m.	Party of 1 Officer 2 N.C.Os and 30 men proceeded to TRAMWAY FARM to continue work on triangle. Commenced work 10.15 p.m. finished 1.15 a.m. 16-3-16.	
			The party had one casualty viz:- 1 man killed whilst riving at 12.30 a.m. 16-3-16.	
			Returned to billets 2.30 a.m. 16/3/16.	
			Weather to-day:- FINE	
			Admissions to Hospital 3 men Discharges from Hospital 1 man Evacuations NIL	
— " —	16/3/16	2 p.m.	Platoons paraded under Platoon Commanders for cleaning of bicycles and rifles.	
		3 p.m.	Company drill	
		4.30 p.m.	Working party consisting of 1 Officer, 10 N.C.Os and 90 men proceeded to RUE ALLEE to continue with trenching. The order for this work was cancelled by C.R.E at 5.30 p.m. and the party was brought back. Returned to billets 7 p.m.	
			Weather to-day:- FINE	
			Admissions to Hospital:- NIL Discharges from Hospital:- NIL Evacuations NIL.	

Sheet No 7   VOLUME 3.

Army Form C. 2118.

WAR DIARY
~~INTELLIGENCE SUMMARY.~~

34th DIVISIONAL COMPANY,
ARMY CYCLIST CORPS.

(Erase heading not required.)

Place	Date	Hour	Summary of Events and Information	Remarks and references to Appendices
CROIX DU BAC	17/3/16	3 am	Working party of 1 Officer 9 N.C.Os and 90 men proceeded to RUE ALLEE to continue work on trenches.	
		6 am to 8 am	170 yards of trench dug 2½ feet wide x 2 feet deep, also 70 yards excavation for parapet of trench, 6 feet wide x 1 foot deep. Party returned to billets.	
		9.30 A.M.	Company drill until 4 p.m.	
		2-30 P.M.	Weather to-day:- FINE Admissions to hospital:- 1 man Discharges from hospital:- NIL Evacuations NIL	
—"—	18/3/16	3 am	Working party of 1 Officer 10 N.C.Os and 80 men proceeded to RUE ALLEE to continue work on trenches	
		6 am to 8 am	140 yards excavation for parapet of trench 6 feet wide x 1 foot deep. 10 men employed putting up 15 Revetting screens including some stays.	
		9.30 am	Party returned to billets	
		2.30 pm	Inspection of Cycles, Rifles and equipment Weather to-day:- very fine Admissions to Hospital:- NIL Discharges from hospital NIL Evacuations NIL	

Sheet No. 8. VOLUME 3.

Army Form C. 2118.

WAR DIARY
or
INTELLIGENCE SUMMARY.
(Erase heading not required.)

**34TH. DIVISIONAL COMPANY,
ARMY CYCLIST CORPS.**

Place	Date	Hour	Summary of Events and Information	Remarks and references to Appendices
CROIX DU BAC	19/3/16	3A.M.	Working party of 1 Officer 8 N.C.Os and 80 men proceeded to RUE ALLEE to continue work on trenches.	
		6A.M. to 8.15A.M.	15 men employed fixing 20 REVETTING SCREENS. 140 yards excavation for parapet of trench 6 feet wide x 1 foot deep	
		9.30A.M	Party returned to billets.	
		3P.M.	Company attended Divine Service in field adjoining billets Weather to-day :- FINE	
			Admissions to Hospital :- NIL. Discharges from Hospital 1 man Evacuations NIL	
-"-	20/3/16	3A.M.	Working party of 1 Officer 9 N.C.Os and 90 men proceeded to RUE ALLEE to continue work on trenches	
		6a.m. to 8 a.m.	Owing to hostile Aircraft only about 1 hours work was actually done.	
		9.30a.m	Party returned to billets	
		2.30p.m.	Physical Drill and Bayonet fighting until 4 p.m. A Party of 1 N.C.O & 5 men, attached to 18th. Bn. N.F. and quartered in a dug out at LA VESEE did about 6 hours work to-day on wiring triangle. 100 pickets put in and 680 yards of barbed wire fixed.	

Sheet No 9. VOLUME 3.

Army Form C. 2118.

WAR DIARY
or
INTELLIGENCE SUMMARY.
(Erase heading not required.)

34TH. DIVISIONAL COMPANY,
ARMY CYCLIST CORPS.

Place	Date	Hour	Summary of Events and Information	Remarks and references to Appendices
CROIX DU BAC.	20/3/16		Weather to-day:- FINE. Admissions to Hospital:- NIL Discharged from Hospital:- NIL Evacuations NIL	
-"-	21/3/16	3A.M.	Working party of 1 Officer 9 N.C.Os and 86 men proceeded to RUE ALLEE to continue work on trenches	
		6A.M. to 8A.M.	160 yards excavation for parapet of trench 6 feet wide × 1 foot deep	
		9-30A.M.	Fixed 15 Revetting Screens. Party returned to billets	
		2.30 P.M.	Platoons paraded under Platoon Commanders for extended order drill Party of 1 N.C.O and 5 men did 6 hours work to-day wiring triangle in front of BOIS GRENIER LINE TRENCH. 100 pickets put in and 680 yards of barbed wire fixed Weather to-day:- FINE Admissions to Hospital:- 2 men Discharged from hospital:- NIL Evacuations:- NIL	
-"-	22/3/16	3A.M.	Working party of 1 Officer 10 N.C.Os and 100 men proceeded to RUE ALLEE to continue work on trenches	
		6A.M. to 8A.M.	200 yards excavation for parapet of trench 6 feet wide × 1 foot deep 20 men employed putting up Revetting Screens	

Sheet No. 10   VOLUME 3

Army Form C. 2118.

WAR DIARY
or
INTELLIGENCE SUMMARY.
(Erase heading not required.)

34TH DIVISIONAL COMPANY, ARMY CYCLIST CORPS.

Place	Date	Hour	Summary of Events and Information	Remarks and references to Appendices
CROIX DU BAC	22/3/16	9.30AM	Party returned to billets	
		2-30pm	Platoons paraded under Platoon Commanders for instruction in Map reading	
			A party of 1 N.C.O. & 5 men were employed for 6 hours at various times to-day wiring triangle. 100 pickets put in and 680 yards of barbed wire fixed. Weather to-day:- Dull, with some rain.	
			Admissions to Hospital 1 man. Discharged from Hospital 1 man. Evacuations 1 man.	
— " —	23/3/16	3AM.	Owing to bad weather work at RUE ALLÉE was cancelled	
		9A.M.	Platoons paraded under Platoon Commanders, for inspection of Bicycles, Rifles, Clothing, Equipment, Gas Helmets &c	
		2-30p.m.	Company drill and musketry until 5 p.m.	
			Party of 1 N.C.O and 5 men were employed for 6 hours to-day in wiring triangle. 100 pickets put in and 680 yards of barbed wire fixed. Weather to-day:- Rain & sleet	
			Admissions to Hospital 1 N.C.O. Discharged from Hospital 1 man. Evacuations- Nil.	

Sheet No. 11   VOLUME 3

WAR DIARY
or
INTELLIGENCE SUMMARY
(Erase heading not required.)

34TH DIVISIONAL COMPANY, ARMY CYCLIST CORPS.

Army Form C. 2118.

Place	Date	Hour	Summary of Events and Information	Remarks and references to Appendices
CROIX DU BAC	24/3/16	3 A.M.	Owing to bad weather work at RUE ALLEE was cancelled	
		9 A.M.	Lecture to Company on Map reading and REPORT writing	
		2-30 P.M.	Company employed cleaning rifles and bicycles. No work done on triangle to-day owing to weather. Weather :- Cold & unsettled with Sleet & snow. Admissions to Hospitals:- NIL. Discharged from Hospital 2 men. Evacuations NIL	
"	25/3/16	3 A.M.	Owing to weather work at RUE ALLEE was again cancelled.	
		9 A.M.	Platoon Commanders lectured their Platoons on Sanitation.	
		2 P.M.	Party of 1 Officer & 25 N.C.Os & men proceeded to DIVISIONAL BATHS at ERQUINGHEM. Weather to-day :- Sleet & Snow. very cold. Admissions to Hospital 1 man. Discharged from Hospital 2 men. Evacuated NIL.	
"	26/3/16	11 A.M.	Company paraded for Divine Service in field adjoining billets.	
		1 P.M.	Company paraded at full strength and proceeded to a field SOUTH of DIVISIONAL HEADQUARTERS to dig practice trenches for bombing purposes	
		6 P.M.	Party returned to billets	
			Weather to-day. Very windy. 1 & 2 showers. Admissions to Hospital :- NIL. Discharged from Hospital:-NIL Evacuations NIL	

Sheet No. 12. VOLUME 3.

Army Form C. 2118

WAR DIARY
or
INTELLIGENCE SUMMARY

(Erase heading not required.)

34TH. DIVISIONAL COMPANY,
ARMY CYCLIST CORPS.

Place	Date	Hour	Summary of Events and Information	Remarks and references to Appendices
CROIX DU BAC	27/3/16	9 A.M. to 6.30 pm	Continued work on practice trenches in two reliefs, consisting of 1 Officer and 50 N.C.Os and men in each relief. Party of 1 N.C.O and 5 men got 6 hours work done to-day wiring TRIANGLE in front of BOIS GRENIER LINE TRENCH. 80 pickets put in, and 2,400 yards of barbed wire fixed. Weather to-day:- showers of rain, with bright intervals.	
		2 p.m.	Party of 1 N.C.O and 25 men went to DIVISIONAL BATHS. Admissions to Hospital :- NIL Discharged from Hospital:- NIL Evacuations NIL	
" "	28/3/16	9 am to 4 pm	Continued work on practice trenches in reliefs. Work stopped owing to rain. Party of 1 N.C.O & 5 men only got one hours work done wiring triangle, owing to shell fire. 60 pickets put in, 300 yards barbed wire fixed. Issue of Gas Helmets to-day. 2nd issue returned to store. Admissions to Hospital:- NIL Discharged from Hospital NIL Evacuations 1 man Weather to-day:- Rain	
" "	29/3/16	3 am	Owing to bad weather work at RUE ALLEE was cancelled.	
		2 pm to 5 pm	Work on practice trenches continued. Party consisted of 1 Officer, 5 N.C.Os and 78 men.	

Sheet 13 VOLUME 3

Army Form C. 2118

WAR DIARY
or
INTELLIGENCE SUMMARY

(Erase heading not required.)

34TH DIVISIONAL COMPANY,
ARMY CYCLIST CORPS.

Place	Date	Hour	Summary of Events and Information	Remarks and references to Appendices
CROIX DU BAC	29/3/16		Weather to-day:- Cloudy, with occasional showers of rain. Admissions to Hospital Nil. Discharged from Hospital Nil. Evacuations Nil.	
-"-	30/3/16	3 A.M.	Working party of 1 Officer, 8 N.C.Os & 100 men proceeded to RUE ALLEE to continue with work on trenches	
		5 A.M. to 8 A.M.	20 men completed a drain for FRONT BORROW PIT which was partly waterlogged. 20 men used for putting up SCREENS. 60 men employed filling in a trench 2ft 6" wide x 6 feet deep 50 yards long	
		9-30 A.M.	Party returned to billets	
		2-30 P.M.	Company drill until 4-30 p.m. Weather:- Fair. Frosty at night. Admissions to Hospital 1 man. Discharged from Hospital Nil. Evacuations Nil.	
-"-	31/3/16	3 A.M.	Working party of 1 Officer, 9 N.C.Os & men proceeded to RUE ALLEE.	
		5-30 A.M. to 7-5 A.M.	Party employed digging up Sods and stacking them	
		8-30 A.M.	Party returned to billets	
		2-30 P.M.	Inspections by Platoon Commanders of rifles, bicycles, Ammunition VC Weather to-day. Fair and bright. Admissions to Hospital Nil. Discharged from Hospital 1 man. Evacuations Nil.	

V.B. Joseph CAPTAIN.
Commdg. 34th. DIV. CYCLISTS.

Sheet I VOLUME 4.

Army Form C. 2118.

34TH DIVISIONAL CORPS.
ARMY CYCLIST CORPS

WAR DIARY
or
INTELLIGENCE SUMMARY.
(Erase heading not required.)

Vol 4

Place	Date	Hour	Summary of Events and Information	Remarks and references to Appendices
CROIX DU BAC.	1/4/16	3 a.m.	A party of 1 Officer 10 N.C.O's & 100 men proceeded to RUE ALLEE for Trenching work. Owing to bad weather work was cancelled.	
		7 a.m.	Party returned to billets.	
		2 p.m. to 4 p.m.	1 hour Physical Drill. 1 hour Company Drill.	
			Admitted to Hospital 1 O.R. Discharged from Hospital NIL Evacuations NIL. Weather:- Rain in forenoon, fair in afternoon.	
do.	2/4/16	3 a.m.	A party of 1 Officer 10 N.C.O's & 90 men proceeded to RUE ALLEE for Trenching.	
		5 a.m. to 7 a.m.	Drained 60 yards of Fire Trench. Framed & puetted 40 yards.	
		9 a.m.	100 yards excavation for parapet dug. Party returned to billets.	
		2.30 p.m.	Platoons paraded under Platoon Commanders for Bayonet-fighting & musketry. Admitted to Hospital NIL. Discharged from Hospital NIL Evacuations NIL. Weather:- Dull with showers at times.	
do.	3/4/16	3 a.m.	A party of 1 Officer 6 NCO's & 30 men proceeded to RUE ALLEE for trenching.	
		5 a.m. to 4 a.m.	Draining Trench and fixing frames. Parapet thickend to 4 feet 6 inches for distance of 60 yards.	

Sheet 2. VOLUME 4.

Army Form C. 2118.

34TH DIVISIONAL COMPANY.
ARMY CYCLIST CORPS.

WAR DIARY
or
INTELLIGENCE SUMMARY
(Erase heading not required.)

Instructions regarding War Diaries and Intelligence Summaries are contained in F.S. Regs., Part II. and the Staff Manual respectively. Title pages will be prepared in manuscript.

Place	Date	Hour	Summary of Events and Information	Remarks and references to Appendices
CROIX DU BAC.	3/4/16	9 a.m.	Party returned to billets.	
		2.30 p.m. to 5 p.m.	Company paraded for inspection of Rifles, Bicycles, Equipment, and Clothing.	
			Admitted to Hospital NIL. Discharged from Hospital NIL. Evacuations NIL.	
			Weather:- Dull with one or two showers.	
do.	4/4/16	9 a.m. to 10 a.m.	Three Platoons proceeded to DIVISIONAL INSTRUCTION SCHOOL for drill purposes in connection with Platoon Commanders Course.	
		11 a.m.	Company paraded for Musketry under Platoon Commanders.	
		2.30 p.m. to 5 p.m.	Company paraded for Company & Extended Order Drill	
		9 p.m.	Reinforcements: 1 O.R. reported for duty from the BASE, and taken on the strength of the Company.	
			Admitted to Hospital NIL. Discharged from Hospital 1 O.R. Evacuations 1 O.R.	
			Weather:- Fine.	
do.	5/4/16	9 a.m. to 12 a.m.	Three Platoons proceeded to DIVISIONAL INSTRUCTION SCHOOL for drill purposes in connection with Platoon Commanders Course.	

Sheet 5. VOLUME 4.

Army Form C. 2118.

34TH DIVISIONAL COMPANY
ARMY CYCLIST CORPS.

WAR DIARY
or
INTELLIGENCE SUMMARY.
(Erase heading not required.)

Place	Date	Hour	Summary of Events and Information	Remarks and references to Appendices
CROIX DU BAC.	5/4/16	2.30 p.m. to 4 p.m.	Company employed overhauling Bicycles and cleaning Rifles. Admitted to Hospital 1 O.R. Discharged from Hospital NIL. Evacuations 1 O.R. Weather:- Fine, but cold.	
do.	6/4/16	9 a.m. to 10 a.m.	Party of 60 NCOs & men at DIVISIONAL INSTRUCTION SCHOOL for drill.	
		9 a.m. to 1 p.m.	The remainder of the Company, with Officers carried out a combined scheme with 34th DIVISIONAL CAVALRY.	
		2.30 p.m.	25 NCOs & men went to DIVISIONAL BATHS at ERQUINGHEM.	
		8.30 p.m. to 10.30 p.m.	A party of 60 NCOs & men went to DIVISIONAL INSTRUCTION SCHOOL to practise a night raid. This was in connection with Platoon Commanders Course. Admitted to Hospital 1 O.R. Discharged from Hospital NIL. Evacuations 1 O.R. Weather:- Very fine.	
do.	7/4/16	9 a.m. to 1 p.m.	Platoons paraded under Platoon Commanders for Physical Drill and Platoon Drill.	
		3 p.m. to 4 p.m.	Lecture on Map reading and report writing.	

Sheet 4. VOLUME 4.

Army Form C. 2118.

34th DIVISIONAL COMPANY
ARMY CYCLIST CORPS.

WAR DIARY
or
INTELLIGENCE SUMMARY

Place	Date	Hour	Summary of Events and Information	Remarks and references to Appendices
CROIX DU BAC.	7/4/16		Admitted to Hospital 1 O.R. Discharged from Hospital NIL Evacuations NIL. Weather :- Very fine.	
do.	8/4/16	9.a.m.	Company Training.	
		2.p.m.	Inspections by Platoon Commanders of Bicycles, Rifles and Ammunition etc.	
		6.p.m.	2/Lieut. Pranked & Sergt. Collins returned from Platoon Commanders Course at DIVISIONAL INSTRUCTION SCHOOL. REINFORCEMENTS & O.R. reported for duty from the BASE & taken on the strength of the Company. Admitted to Hospital NIL Discharged from Hospital NIL Evacuations NIL. Weather :- Dull, but dry.	
do.	9/4/16	3.p.m.	Company attended Divine Service in field adjoining billets. Admitted to Hospital NIL Discharged from Hospital NIL Evacuations NIL. Weather :- Fair and Bright.	
do.	10/4/16	9.a.m. to 1.p.m.	Training under Platoon Commanders. Instruction in Guard Mounting Parades & Extended order drill.	
		2.30pm to 5.p.m.	Platoons practised Relay System of delivering messages. The 2nd DIVISION AUSTRALIAN CYCLIST COMPANY relieved our Guard on Coal Dump at BAC. ST. MAUR at 6.p.m.	

Sheet 5 VOLUME 4.

Army Form C. 2118.

Instructions regarding War Diaries and Intelligence Summaries are contained in F. S. Regs., Part II. and the Staff Manual respectively. Title pages will be prepared in manuscript.

WAR DIARY
or
INTELLIGENCE SUMMARY.
(Erase heading not required.)

34TH DIVISIONAL COMPANY
ARMY CYCLIST CORPS.

Place	Date	Hour	Summary of Events and Information	Remarks and references to Appendices
CROIX DU BAC.	10/4/16		Admitted to Hospital NIL Discharged from Hospital NIL Evacuations NIL. Weather :- Fair, rather Cloudy.	
do.	11/4/16	9.a.m.	Company preparing for move; cleaning billets &c.	
		1.p.m.	The 2nd AUSTRALIAN DIVISIONAL CYCLIST COMPANY took over our billets.	
		2.p.m.	Moved to SEC-BOIS, where we arrived at 4 p.m. and went into billets for the night in barns quite close to the village. 2/Lieut J.L. BURTT proceeded on 8 days leave to England. Admitted to Hospital NIL Discharged from Hospital NIL Evacuations NIL. Weather :- Overcast, with occasional passing showers. Very windy.	
SEC. BOIS	12/4/16	6.a.m.	Company paraded and proceeded to SAINT MARTIN, about 1 mile West of SAINT OMER. where we arrived at 4.30 p.m. & took over billets. Admitted to Hospital NIL Discharged from Hospital NIL Evacuations 1 O.R. Weather :- Rain & very windy.	
SAINT MARTIN	13/4/16	9.a.m.	Company employed putting billets in order.	
		2.p.m.	Inspection by Platoon Commanders of Cycles & Rifles. Admitted to Hospital 1 O.R. Discharged from Hospital NIL. Evacuations NIL Weather :- Showers with fair intervals.	

Sheet 6. VOLUME. 4.

Army Form C. 2118.

34TH DIVISIONAL COMPANY
ARMY CYCLIST CORPS.

WAR DIARY
or
INTELLIGENCE SUMMARY.

(Erase heading not required.)

Place	Date	Hour	Summary of Events and Information	Remarks and references to Appendices
SAINT MARTIN	14/4/16	6.45 a.m. to 7.30 a.m.	Physical Drill	
		9 a.m. to 4 p.m.	Platoons paraded under Platoon Commanders and proceeded to reconnoitre all roads due West of ST MARTIN as far as QUERCAMPS. Admitted to Hospital NIL Discharged from Hospital NIL Evacuations NIL. Weather :- Cool with showers.	
do.	15/4/16	6.45 a.m. to 7.30 a.m.	Physical Drill.	
		9 a.m. to 12 noon.	Company employed overhauling & cleaning Cycles. Admissions to Hospital NIL. Discharges from Hospital NIL Evacuations NIL. Weather :- Fair & Cool.	
do.	16/4/16		The Company paraded at full strength for Inspection of Kit and Equipment - Admitted to Hospital NIL Discharged from Hospital 1 O.R. Evacuations NIL. Weather :- Cool with Showers.	
do.	19/4/16	6.45 a.m. to 7.30 a.m.	Physical Drill	
		9 a.m. to 5 p.m.	Company paraded and proceeded to RIFLE RANGE, 1 mile N.W. of ST Martin and carried out a "Grouping Practice" - 5 rounds per man. Admitted to Hospital NIL. Discharged from Hospital NIL Evacuations NIL. Weather :- Overcast, with occasional rain.	

Army Form C. 2118.

WAR DIARY
or
INTELLIGENCE SUMMARY.

(Erase heading not required.)

Sheet of VOLUME 4.

34TH. DIVISIONAL COMPANY
ARMY CYCLIST CORPS.

Instructions regarding War Diaries and Intelligence Summaries are contained in F. S. Regs., Part II. and the Staff Manual respectively. Title pages will be prepared in manuscript.

Place	Date	Hour	Summary of Events and Information	Remarks and references to Appendices
SAINT-MARTIN	18/4/16	6.45 a.m. to 7.30 a.m.	Physical Drill.	
		9 a.m. to 1 p.m.	Casuals in musketry proceeded to RANGE under Musketry Officer & fired Grouping Practice.	
		2.30 p.m. to 6 p.m.	Company employed preparing for move. Admitted to Hospital NIL. Discharged from Hospital NIL. Evacuations NIL. Weather:- Dry & very windy.	
REBERGUES	19/4/16		Company moved into Billets in Farmhouses at REBERGUES 12 miles due West of St Martin and attached to 2nd CAVALRY DIVISION to undergo a course of training in the work of Divisional Mounted Troops. Admitted to Hospital NIL. Discharged from Hospital NIL. Evacuations NIL. Weather:- Very stormy, with rain.	
do.	20/4/16	8 a.m. to 1 p.m.	Officers & Sergeants of the Company attended lecture and practical demonstration on Patrol Work in Conjunction with Cavalry.	
		2.30 p.m. to 5 p.m.	Lecture by G.O.C. 2nd Cavalry Division on work of Divisional Mounted Troops. Admitted to Hospital NIL. Discharged from Hospital NIL. Evacuations NIL. Weather:- Rain & very windy.	

Sheet 8. VOLUME 4.

Army Form C. 2118.

34th DIVISIONAL COMPANY.
ARMY CYCLIST CORPS

WAR DIARY
or
INTELLIGENCE SUMMARY.
(Erase heading not required.)

Instructions regarding War Diaries and Intelligence Summaries are contained in F.S. Regs., Part II. and the Staff Manual respectively. Title pages will be prepared in manuscript.

Place	Date	Hour	Summary of Events and Information	Remarks and references to Appendices
REBECQUES	21/4/16	8 a.m. to 2:30 p.m.	Officers & Sergeants of the Company with 60 N.C.O.s & men carried out "Rear Guard Scheme" in conjunction with DIVISIONAL CAVALRY in the vicinity of LUMBRES.	
		3:30 p.m.	Officers & Sergeants attended a Lecture by CAPT. NICHOLSON, 2nd Cavalry Division at JOURNAY on the above scheme.	
			Admitted to Hospital NIL. Discharged from Hospital NIL. Evacuations NIL. Weather:- Stormy & heavy showers.	
do.	22/4/16		Scheme for to-day cancelled owing to bad weather.	
			Admitted to Hospital NIL. Discharged from Hospital NIL. Evacuations NIL. Weather:- Very heavy rain.	
do.	23/4/16	9 a.m. to 11 a.m.	Company employed cleaning Bicycles and Rifles.	
		2 p.m. 3 p.m.	Inspection of Rifles & Cycles by Platoon Commanders.	
		5 p.m.	Lecture at JOURNAY to Officers & Sergeants on Scheme to be carried out next day.	
			Admitted to Hospital NIL. Discharged from Hospital NIL. Evacuations NIL. Weather:- Very fine.	
do.	24/4/16	8 a.m.	Officers & Sergeants & three Platoons carried out "Advanced Guard" Scheme in conjunction with 34th DIVISIONAL CAVALRY in the vicinity of ESCOEUILLES and LICQUES.	
			Admitted to Hospital NIL. Discharged from Hospital NIL. Evacuations NIL. Weather:- Very fine.	

Sheet 9. VOLUME 4

Army Form C. 2118.

34TH. DIVISIONAL COMPANY.
ARMY CYCLIST CORPS.

WAR DIARY
or
INTELLIGENCE SUMMARY.

(Erase heading not required.)

Place	Date	Hour	Summary of Events and Information	Remarks and references to Appendices
REBERGUES	25/4/16	9 a.m.	Officers & Sergeants & three Platoons carried out an "OUTPOST" Scheme with Cavalry at LA QUINGOIE. Admitted to Hospital NIL. Discharged from Hospital NIL. Evacuations NIL. Weather :- Very fine.	
do.	26/4/16	8 a.m.	Officers & Sergeants & three Platoons along with Cavalry practised the working of PATROLS. Admitted to Hospital NIL. Discharged from Hospital NIL. Evacuations NIL. Weather :- Still very fine.	
do.	27/4/16	8.30 a.m.	Officers & Sergeants & three Platoons along with Cavalry practised Attacks on a wood and village.	
		4 p.m.	Lecture on above scheme at JOURNAY. Admitted to Hospital NIL. Discharged from Hospital NIL. Evacuations NIL. Weather :- Very fine.	
do.	28/4/16	8 a.m.	Officers & Sergeants & three Platoons along with Cavalry carried out a "Flank Guard" Scheme.	
		5 p.m.	Lecture at JOURNY on above scheme also in the Collecting of Information and dealing with Prisoners of War. Admitted to Hospital NIL. Discharged from Hospital NIL. Evacuations 1 O.R. Weather :- Very fine.	

Sheet 10. VOLUME 4

Army Form C. 2118
34TH. DIVISIONAL COMPANY,
ARMY CYCLIST CORPS.

WAR DIARY
or
INTELLIGENCE SUMMARY

(Erase heading not required.)

Place	Date	Hour	Summary of Events and Information	Remarks and references to Appendices
REBERGUES	29/4/16	8 a.m.	Staff ride for Officers & N.C.O's of Cyclists & Cavalry. Scheme - Advance Guard.	
		1 p.m.	2nd Cavalry Division Course finished.	
			2. O.R. Proceeded on eight days' leave to England.	
			Admitted to Hospital NIL. Discharged from Hospital NIL. Evacuations NIL.	
			Weather:- Very fine.	
	30/4/16	9 a.m.	Company employed cleaning Bicycles & Rifles.	
		11 a.m.	Inspection by Platoon Commanders of Bicycles & Rifles.	
			Admitted to Hospital NIL. Discharged from Hospital NIL. Evacuations NIL.	

V.S. Japp Capt
Comdg 34th Div Cyclist Coy

Sheet No. 1. Volume 5.

34th Divisional Company
Army Cyclist Corps.

Army Form C. 2118.

Vol 5

WAR DIARY
INTELLIGENCE SUMMARY

Instructions regarding War Diaries and Intelligence Summaries are contained in F. S. Regs., Part II and the Staff Manual respectively. Title pages will be prepared in manuscript.

(Erase heading not required.)

Place	Date	Hour	Summary of Events and Information	Remarks and references to Appendices
REBERQUES	1/5/16		Company left REBERQUES and proceeded to ST. MARTIN au LAERT. Reinforcements:- 7 O.R. reported for duty were taken on strength of Company. Weather:- Very fine.	
ST. MARTIN au LAERT.	2/5/16	6 am to 1 pm. 3 pm.	Company paraded and took part in a Divisional Service in the vicinity of ST. MARTIN. Inspection by Platoon Commanders of Rifles, Ammunition, etc. Weather:- Generally fine; short thunderstorm during afternoon.	
-"-	3/5/16	8 am to 2.30 pm. 8.30 pm.	Company paraded and took part in a Divisional Service in the vicinity of ST. MARTIN. Strength Decrease:- Lieut. J. Wynne-Morley invalided to England and struck off strength of Company. O. Rnks. of 1 Officer, 8 N.C.O's and 30 men entrained at ST. OMER for LONGEAU for duty under R.T.O. LONGEAU. Weather: Fine.	
-"-	4/5/16	5.30 pm.	Company, less one Platoon, on duty at LONGEAU, entrained at ST. OMER for LONGEAU. One Officer, 33 O.R. employed on detraining duties at LONGEAU under R.T.O. Weather:- Very fine.	

Sheet No. 2 Volume 5.

Army Form C. 2118

34th Divl. Company.
Army Cyclist Corps

WAR DIARY
or
INTELLIGENCE SUMMARY
(Erase heading not required.)

Instructions regarding War Diaries and Intelligence Summaries are contained in F.S. Regs., Part II and the Staff Manual respectively. Title Pages will be prepared in manuscript.

Place	Date	Hour	Summary of Events and Information	Remarks and references to Appendices
ST. MARTIN au LAERT.	5/5/16	4 a.m.	Company, less one platoon, detrained at LONGEAU to and proceeded to BRESLE.	
		11 a.m.	Arrived at BRESLE and took over billets. One officer, 33 O.R. employed on detraining duties at LONGEAU. Weather :- fine.	
BRESLE	6/5/16	9 a.m.	Company employed in cleaning up billets.	
		11	Rifle and Cycle Inspection by Platoon Commanders.	
		12 noon.	Party of one officer, 30 O.R. proceeded to MOULIN de VIVIER for duty with 34th Divl. Signal Company.	
		2 p.m.	One officer, 33 O.R. employed on detraining duties at LONGEAU under R.T.O.	
		4 p.m.	2 O.R. returned from leave to England and resumed duty with Company.	
		7 p.m.		
"	7/5/16		1 Officer 30 O.R. working at MOULIN de VIVIER digging trenches 2'x 6' for laying Artillery cables. 1 officer 33 O.R. upon completing detraining duties at LONGEAU returned for duty with company. Weather :- Rain.	
"	8/5/16		1 Officer 30 O.R. working at MOULIN de VIVIER, digging trenches 2'x 6' for laying Artillery cables.	

Sheet No. 3, Volume 5.

Army Form C. 2118

WAR DIARY
or
INTELLIGENCE SUMMARY

34th Divisional Company
Army Cyclist Corps

(Erase heading not required.)

Instructions regarding War Diaries and Intelligence Summaries are contained in F. S. Regs., Part II. and the Staff Manual respectively. Title Pages will be prepared in manuscript.

Place	Date	Hour	Summary of Events and Information	Remarks and references to Appendices
BRESLE	8/5/16		20 O.R. joined about party at MOULIN de VIVIER. 2 N.C.O's & 5 men detailed for Road Control on ALBERT - AMIENS main road under A.P.M. 34th Division. Weather :- Rain.	
BRESLE and BÉHENCOURT	9/5/16	9 a.m.	2 N.C.O.'s and men returned from road control duties & resumed duty with Coy. Company, less 1 officer & 50 O.R. proceeded to ALBERT for entrenching under C.R.E. 34th Division.	
		7 p.m.	1 Officer, 50 O.R. continued work at MOULIN de VIVIER. Company, less 1 officer & 50 O.R. moved into billets at BÉHENCOURT. Weather :- Fine, occasional showers.	
BÉHENCOURT.	10/5/16		1 Officer 50 O.R. continued work at MOULIN de VIVIER. 1 Officer 2 O.R. proceeded on leave to ENGLAND.	
		11 a.m.	Rifle, cycle, and equipment inspection by Platoon Commanders.	
		7 p.m.	Company, less 1 officer & 50 O.R. proceeded to ALBERT for entrenching under C.R.E. 34th Division. Weather :- very fine.	
"	11/5/16	7 a.m.	1 Officer 50 O.R. continued work at MOULIN de VIVIER. Company, less 1 officer, 50. O.R. proceeded to ALBERT for entrenching under C.R.E. 34th Division.	

Sheet No 4, Volume 5

Army Form C. 2118

WAR DIARY
or
INTELLIGENCE SUMMARY

(Erase heading not required.)

34th Divisional Company
Army Cyclist Corps.

Place	Date	Hour	Summary of Events and Information	Remarks and references to Appendices
BÉHENCOURT	11/5/16		5. O.R. proceeded to (Albert) ALBERT, 4 as Divisional Snipers, 1 as cook. Weather: Cold, with showers.	
BÉHENCOURT and BEAUCOURT	12/5/16	11 am	1 Officer, 50. O.R. continued work at MOULIN du VIVIER Company, less 2 Officers 57 O.R. proceeded to and occupied billets at BEAUCOURT. Weather: Fair.	
BEAUCOURT	13/5/16	11 am	One Officer, 50. O.R. continued work at MOULIN du VIVIER.	
"		3 pm	Cycle, rifle, and equipment inspection by Platoon Commanders. Inspection of billets by Platoon Commanders. Admissions to Hospital :- 1 O.R. Weather: Rain.	
"	14/5/16	11 am	One Officer, 50 O.R. continued work at MOULIN du VIVIER. Billet & kit inspection by Platoon Commanders. Weather :- Stormy.	
"	15/5/16	9.30 am	One Officer 50 O.R. continued work at MOULIN du VIVIER. Lectures on "Map Reading" and "Yaoitin" by Platoon Commanders. Weather :- Wet.	

Sheet No. 5. Volume 5.

Army Form C. 2118

Instructions regarding War Diaries and Intelligence Summaries are contained in F. S. Regs., Part II. and the Staff Manual respectively. Title Pages will be prepared in manuscript.

WAR DIARY or INTELLIGENCE SUMMARY

34th Divisional Company
Army Cyclist Corps.

(Erase heading not required.)

Place	Date	Hour	Summary of Events and Information	Remarks and references to Appendices
BEAUCOURT.	16/5/16	9.30am	One Officer 50 O.R. continued work at MOULIN de VIVIER. Platoons paraded under Platoon Commanders for Physical Training & Bayonet Fighting.	
		2.30pm	Training in Cyclists' duties under Platoon Commanders. Weather :- Very fine.	
"	17/5/16		One Officer 50 O.R. continued work at MOULIN de VIVIER.	
		10 am	Kit Inspection by Platoon Commanders.	
		11 am	Cycle and rifle inspection by Platoon Commanders.	
		2.30pm	Physical Training & Bayonet fighting under Platoon Commanders. Admitted to Hospital :- 3 O.R. Weather :- Very fine.	
"	18/5/16		One Officer, 50 O.R. continued work at MOULIN de VIVIER. 1 Officer 2 O.R. returned from leave to England resumed duty with Company.	
		9.30 am	Cyclist Training under Platoon Commanders.	
		2.30pm	Physical Training & Bayonet fighting under Platoon Commanders. Weather :- Very fine.	
"	19/5/16		1 Officer 23 O.R. continued work at MOULIN de VIVIER. 27 O.R. returned from MOULIN de VIVIER for duty with Company.	

1375 Wt. W593/826 1,000,000 4/15 J.B.C. & A. A.D.S.S./Forms/C. 2118.

Sheet No 6. Volume 5.   Army Form C. 2118

WAR DIARY
or
~~INTELLIGENCE SUMMARY~~

34th Divisional Company
Army Cyclist Corps.

Place	Date	Hour	Summary of Events and Information	Remarks and references to Appendices
BEAUCOURT.	19/5/16	9.30 am	Musketry & Visual training under Platoon Commanders	
		2.30 pm	Lateral communication under Platoon Commanders. Discharged from Hospital :- 2 O.R. Weather :- very fine.	
"	20/5/16		One Officer 23 O.R. continued work at MOULIN du VIVIER	
		9.30 am	Inspection of Platoons under Platoon Commanders for purpose of selecting N.C.O's and men to be transferred to Infantry. Weather :- Very fine.	
"	21/5/16		One Officer, 18 O.R. continued work at MOULIN du VIVIER.	
		9.15 am	Church Parade.	
		11 am.	Cycle and rifle inspection under Platoon Commanders. 5 O.R. returned from MOULIN du VIVIER and resumed duty with Company Weather :- very fine.	
"	22/5/16		One Officer 18 O.R continued work at MOULIN du VIVIER.	
		9.30 am	Inspection of draft of 83 O.R (by the O.C) - to be transferred to Infantry & to the Base.	
		2.30 pm	Kit Inspection under Platoon Commanders. Weather :- Fine. Admissions to Hospital :- 1 O.R.	

Sheet No 7 Volume 5

Army Form C. 2118

WAR DIARY
or
INTELLIGENCE SUMMARY

34th Divisional Company Army Cyclist Corps

Instructions regarding War Diaries and Intelligence Summaries are contained in F. S. Regs., Part II. and the Staff Manual respectively. Title Pages will be prepared in manuscript.

(Erase heading not required.)

Place	Date	Hour	Summary of Events and Information	Remarks and references to Appendices
BEAUCOURT.	23/5/16		One officer 18 O.R. continued work at MOULIN de VIVIER.	
		1 pm	Draft of 88 O.R. despatched to BRESLE to join 24th Bn. Northumberland Fusiliers, upon being transferred to that unit for duty.	
"	24/5/16	11 am	One Officer 18 O.R. continued work at MOULIN de VIVIER.	
		8 am	2 Officers, 5 O.R. proceeded to HEILLY to entrain for Base as first reinforcements.	
		9.30 am	21. O.R. noodnaming under Camp Commandant, III Corps.	
		2.30 pm	Cyclist training under Platoon Commanders.	
			Musketry and Visual Training under Platoon Commanders.	
			Weather :- Stormy	
"	25/5/16		One Officer 18 O.R. continued work at MOULIN de VIVIER.	
		10.30 am	Company paraded at full strength for inspection by O.C.	
		1 pm	24. O.R. proceeded to FRECHENCOURT for fatigue work under R.T.O.	
		1.30 pm	12 O.R. proceeded to FRECHENCOURT WOOD to procure picketing posts and pegs. for III Corps.	
			Weather :- Stormy.	
"	26/5/16	9 am	One Officer 18 O.R. continued work at MOULIN de VIVIER.	
			6 O.R. Regimental Fatigue duty	
		7.45 am	21 O.R. Roadrepairing at BEAUCOURT under Camp Commandant.	

Sheet No 8. Volume 5.

Army Form C. 2118

Instructions regarding War Diaries and Intelligence Summaries are contained in F. S. Regs., Part II. and the Staff Manual respectively. Title Pages will be prepared in manuscript.

WAR DIARY
or
INTELLIGENCE SUMMARY

(Erase heading not required.)

34th Divisional Company
Army Cyclist Corps.

Place	Date	Hour	Summary of Events and Information	Remarks and references to Appendices
BEAUCOURT.	26/5/16	8.30am	6. O.R. for fatigue under Supply Officer at BEAUCOURT.	
		9.45am	11 O.R. proceeded to FRECHENCOURT for fatigue work under R.T.O.	
			Weather :- fine.	
"	27/5/16	7.45am	1 Officer 18 O.R. continued work at MOULIN de VIVIER	
		8.16am	1 N.C.O. in charge of watering party under Camp Commandant, BEAUCOURT.	
			6 O.R. fatigue duty under Supply Officer III Corps.	
		7 am.	5 O.R. Regimental Fatigue duty	
		9.30am	Musketry under Platoon Commanders.	
			Weather :- fine.	
"	28/5/16	7.45am	1 Officer 18 O.R. continued work at MOULIN de VIVIER.	
			20 O.R. fatigue duty under Camp Commandant, BEAUCOURT.	
		9.30am	Church Parade.	
		2.30pm	Battalion Kit Inspection by O.C.	
			Weather :- Fine	
"	29/5/16	7am	1 Officer 18 O.R. continued work at MOULIN de VIVIER.	
			Regimental Fatigue.	
		10.30am	Company Drill.	
		2.30pm	Platoon Drill under Platoon Commanders	
			Weather :- Fine	

Sheet No 9. Volume 5.

Army Form C. 2118

34th Divisional Company
Army Cyclist Corps.

WAR DIARY
or
INTELLIGENCE SUMMARY
(Erase heading not required.)

Place	Date	Hour	Summary of Events and Information	Remarks and references to Appendices
BEAUCOURT.	30/5/16	6.30am	One Officer 18 O.R. continued work at MOULIN de VIVIER.	
			6 O.R. Regimental Fatigue.	
		10.30am	Battalion Drill under Adjutant.	
		2.30pm	Platoon Drill under Platoon Commanders.	
			Weather :- Fine.	
"	31/5/16		One Officer 18 O.R. continued work at MOULIN de VIVIER.	
		7.15am	Physical Training	
		10.30am	Company Drill under Adjutant.	
		2.30pm	Platoon Drill under Platoon Commanders.	
			Weather :- Fine	
			Detachment :-	
	1/6/16		10 O.R. attached to 34th Division Signal Coy.	
	3/5/16			
	11/5/16		4 O.R. attached to 34th Division as Snipers	
	31/5/16		1 " " " Cook to Divisional Snipers.	

France
31-5-16

W.E. Nash Lieut.
for O.C. 34th Divisional Company
A.C.C.

www.ingramcontent.com/pod-product-compliance
Lightning Source LLC
Chambersburg PA
CBHW081248170426
43191CB00037B/2078